THANK YOU

and

Other Poems

THANK YOU

and

Other Poems

by

Kenneth Koch

GROVE PRESS, INC.   NEW YORK

Second printing

Acknowledgments — A number of these poems were previously published in the following books and periodicals: *A New Folder*, *Art News*, *Between Worlds*, *Big Table*, *Evergreen Review*, *Folder*, *i.e.*, *Locus Solus*, *The New American Poetry 1945–1960* (Grove Press, 1960), *Nomad*, *Partisan Review*, *Permanently* (Tiber Press, 1961), *Poems* De Nagy, 1953), *Poetry*, *Quarterly Review of Literature*, *Semicolon*.

Manufactured in the United States of America

CONTENTS

THANK YOU

and

Other Poems

ON THE GREAT ATLANTIC RAINWAY

I set forth one misted white day of June
Beneath the great Atlantic rainway, and heard:
"Honestly you smite worlds of truth, but
Lose your own trains of thought, like a pigeon.
Did you once ride in Kenneth's machine?"
"Yes, I rode there, an old man in shorts, blind,
Who had lost his way in the filling station; Kenneth was kind."
"Did he fill your motionless ears with resonance and stain?"
"No, he spoke not as a critic, but as a man."
"Tell me, what did he say?" "He said,
'My eyes are the white sky, the gravel on the groundway my sad
    lament.' "
"And yet he drives between the two. . . ." "Exactly, Jane,

And that is the modern idea of fittingness,
To, always in motion, lose nothing, although beneath the
Rainway they move in threes and twos completely
Ruined for themselves, like moving pictures."
"But how other?" "Formulalessness, to go from the sun
Into love's sweet disrepair. He would fondly express
'Rain trees'—which is not a poem, 'rain trees. . . .' "
"Still, it is mysterious to have an engine
That floats bouquets! and one day in the rear-vision
Mirror of his car we vowed delight,
The insufficiency of the silverware in the sunlight,
The dreams he steals from and smiles, losing gain."

"Yet always beneath the rainway unsyntactical
Beauty might leap up!" "That we might sing
From smiles' ravines, 'Rose, the reverse of everything,
May be profaned or talked at like a hat.' "
"Oh that was sweet and short, like the minuet
Of stars, which would permit us to seem our best friends
By silver's eminent lights! For nature is so small, ends
Falsely reign, distending the time we did
Behind our hope for body-work, riding with Kenneth."
Their voicing ceased, then started again, to complain
That we are offered nothing when it starts to rain
In the same way, though we are dying for the truth.

SUMMERY WEATHER

One earring's smile
Near the drawer
And at night we gambling
At that night the yacht on Venice
Glorious too, oh my heavens
See how her blouse was starched up.
"The stars reminded me of youse."
"His lip sticks out. His eye is sailing.
I don't care what happens
Now," she says,
"After those winters in Florida!"
As for a pure dance
With oranges,
"All my factories
Need refilling,"
The corpse said, falling down between them.
"Okay okay
Here's a banana and a bandana
The light on a bright night,
With which, to finish, my personal challenge."
Oh how she admired him!
Lovely are fireworks;
Given, the shirts have a sale
To themselves; but
The wind is blowing, blowing!

THE BRASSIERE FACTORY

Is the governor falling
From a great height?
Arm in arm we fled the brassiere factory,
The motion-boat stayed on the shore!
I saw how round its bottom was
As you walked into southern France—
Upon the light hair of an arm
Cigar bands lay!
I kissed you then. Oh is my bar
The insect of your will? The water rose,
But will the buffalo on
The nickel yet be still?
For how can windows hold out the light
In your eyes!
Darling, we fled the brassiere factory
In forty-eight states,
Arm in arm,
When human beings hung on us
And you had been arrested by the cloths
Were used in making, and I said, "The Goths
Know such delight," but still we fled, away
Into a dinner atmosphere
From all we knew, and fall asleep this day.
O maintenance men, with cruel eyes,
Then arm in arm we fled the listless factory!
The music changed your fingers' ends to pearl,
I punched you, you foolish girl,
For thanks to the metronome we got out alive, in the air
Where the sun filled us with cruelty!
There's what to do
Except despair, like pages! and laugh
Like prawns, about the sea!
Oh arm in arm we fled the industry
Into an earth of banks
And foolish tanks, for what bare breasts might be.

THE BRICKS

The bricks in a wall
Sang this song
"We shall not fall
The whole day long
But white and small
Lie in abandon."

Then the fair maid
Passed with her love
And she to him said,
"There are stars above
Where they have been laid
Let us lie in abandon."

Then the wolf came
With his teeth in abandon
And the lion came
With his teeth in abandon
And they ravaged and he came
To the white stone

And he kissed the field's grass
And he lay in abandon.
"I forget if she was
Or he was the stone
Of if it was the animals,"
And, "Everything comes soon."

JANUARY NINETEENTH

1

Houses do not fail to sing in a ghostly way among themselves.
"I felt foolish in the fishmarket of white horses." "She hands me the
pleasant nucleus."
"The French parliament have grouped themselves around silence."
Yes, the houses sing!
"The ear sails itself into the wintry custom of door telephones!" Wintry
lake!
Bassinets leak through the covers of ice-dripping magazines
Of Clark Bar kindness, in the midst of Romeo My Telegraph Street.
Like a wheel of cigars
Unfinished by Perseus, the coconut bra parts with chilblains
The unbanished sidewalk, where secret members of the Tear walk. O
boisterousness!
"She wears a tiara of idleness, she has cocoa on her chair-bonnet;
Each of her children is worth sixteen dollars a million, her hat is in
Nebraska;
Her feet are in South Fort Worth, Texas, and the ale manufacturers
Are agreed to cut criss-crosses in green upon the lilac statue of her
milliner—"
So—"my strength!"
"The cheerleaders have penciled the bathtubs with the words 'Maine
State'
So as not to be bothered by her prettiness, her booths have become a
sidewalk, her eyes a dove
On the cover of Plinth Magazine, and her groceries the weather
In red and green; the weather is costly and marvelous!" The shoe
slips, and the eye comes, off,
But the basket of circuses is still free on the arm of the sanctified circus
deliverer,
Whose swift speeches cancel our leaves for seventy weeks. "Bakery of
coffee gloves!
Oh Lorna Doone fizzled the dazzling icicle-pencil
By sheer blue shirts." My hill! "Let's turn to the pathway of potatoes!"

2

Buttes-Chaumont pleased Aragon; the fire department say, "Flint is
  our religion."
The bone Andes are still pledging facial Switzerland to Peruvian
  intestinal prisms
Too coffee-like to replace the face; but then that tissue paper is their
  business. Our replica
Of all this is the sunset, a basilica of friendly brassieres—
The government of Switzerland may not be overcome by gonorrhea!
Finland wants "boats." The sheep want to go to Finland.
"Sand will not make you a very thrilling overcoat," the house said to me;
Our peach tree sat down. "Chalk was dreaming of the lightning and
  thunder."

The hilt of the swords! the hilt of the swords!
The sheep tree, the lightning and thunder!
Powder writes another novel to itself:
Passengers, adroit pyramids, and blue triremes!
Oh how I hate to "Gogol"! Now, baby sweater!
The Green Cab Sighs have fallen in love.

DESIRE FOR SPRING

Calcium days, days when we feed our bones!
Iron days, which enrich our blood!
Saltwater days, which give us valuable iodine!
When will there be a perfectly ordinary spring day?
For my heart needs to be fed, not my urine
Or my brain, and I wish to leap to Pittsburgh
From Tuskegee, Indiana, if necessary, spreading like a flower
In the spring light, and growing like a silver stair.
Nothing else will satisfy me, not even death!
Not even broken life insurance policies, cancer, loss of health,
Ruined furniture, prostate disease, headaches, melancholia,
No, not even a ravaging wolf eating up my flesh!
I want spring, I want to turn like a mobile
In a new fresh air! I don't want to hibernate
Between walls, between halls! I want to bear
My share of the anguish of being succinctly here!
Not even moths in the spell of the flame
Can want it to be warmer so much as I do!
Not even the pilot slipping into the great green sea
In flames can want less to be turned to an icicle!
Though admiring the icicle's cunning, how shall I be satisfied
With artificial daisies and roses, and wax pears?
O breeze, my lovely, come in, that I mayn't be stultified!
Dear coolness of heaven, come swiftly and sit in my chairs!

TO YOU

I love you as a sheriff searches for a walnut
That will solve a murder case unsolved for years
Because the murderer left it in the snow beside a window
Through which he saw her head, connecting with
Her shoulders by a neck, and laid a red
Roof in her heart. For this we live a thousand years;
For this we love, and we live because we love, we are not
Inside a bottle, thank goodness! I love you as a
Kid searches for a goat; I am crazier than shirttails
In the wind, when you're near, a wind that blows from
The big blue sea, so shiny so deep and so unlike us;
I think I am bicycling across an Africa of green and white fields
Always, to be near you, even in my heart
When I'm awake, which swims, and also I believe that you
Are trustworthy as the sidewalk which leads me to
The place where I again think of you, a new
Harmony of thoughts! I love you as the sunlight leads the prow
Of a ship which sails
From Hartford to Miami, and I love you
Best at dawn, when even before I am awake the sun
Receives me in the questions which you always pose.

AUS EINER KINDHEIT

Is the basketball coach a homosexual lemon manufacturer? It is
suspected by O'Ryan in his submarine.
When I was a child we always cried to be driven for a ride in that
submarine. Daddy would say Yes!
Mommy would say No! The maid read *Anna Karenina* and told us
secrets. Some suspected her of a liaison with O'Ryan. Nothing but
squirrels
Seemed to be her interest, at the windows, except on holidays, like
Easter and Thanksgiving, when
She would leave the basement and rave among the leaves, shouting, I
am the Spirit of Softball! Come to me!
Daddy would always leave town. And a chorus of spiders
Would hang from my bedroom wall. Mommy had a hat made out of
pasty hooks. She gave a party to limburger cheese.
We all were afraid that O'Ryan would come!
He came, he came! as the fall wind comes, waving and razing and
swirling the leaves
With his bags, his moustache, his cigar, his golfball, his pencils, his
April compasses, and over his whole
Body we children saw signs of life beneath the water! Oh!
Will he dance the hornpipe? we wondered, Will he smoke a cigar
underneath eleven inches of ocean? Will he beat the pavement
Outside our door with his light feet, for being so firm? Is he a lemon
Memnon?
O'Ryan O'Ryan O'Ryan! The maid came up from the basement, we
were all astonished. And she said, "Is it Thanksgiving? Christmas?
I felt
A force within me stir." And then she saw O'Ryan! The basketball
coach followed her up from the cellar. He and O'Ryan fight!
No one is homosexual then! happily I swim through the bathtubs with
my scarlet-haired sister
Z. ("O women I love you!" O'Ryan cried.) And we parked under
water. Then, looking out the window,
We saw that snow had begun to fall, upon the green grass, and both shyly
entered the new world of our bleached underwear. Rome! Rome!
Was our maid entertaining that limburger cheese, or my mother? has
the passageway fallen asleep? and can one's actions for six years be
called "improper"?

I hope not. I hope the sea. I hope cigars will be smoked. I hope it from New York to California. From Tallahassee to St. Paul.

I hope the orange punching bag will be socked, and that you'll be satisfied, sweet friend. I hope international matrimony, lambent skies, and "Ship, ahoy!"

For we're due to be dawned on, I guess.

SPRING

Let's take a walk
In the city
Till our shoes get wet
(It's been raining
All night) and when
We see the traffic
Lights and the moon
Let's take a smile
Off the ashcan, let's walk
Into town (I mean
A lemon peel)

Let's make music
(I hear the cats
Purply beautiful
Like hallways in summer
Made of snowing rubber
Valence piccalilli and diamonds)
Oh see the arch ruby
Of this late March sky
Are you less intelligent
Than the pirate of lemons
Let's take a walk

I know you tonight
As I have never known
A book of white stones
Or a bookcase of orange groans
Or symbolism
I think I'm in love
With those imaginary racetracks
Of red traced grey in
The sky and the gimcracks
Of all you know and love
Who once loathed firecrackers
And license plates and
Diamonds but now you love them all
And just for my sake

Let's take a walk
Into the river
(I can even do that
Tonight) where
If I kiss you please
Remember with your shoes off
You're so beautiful like
A lifted umbrella orange
And white we may never
Discover the blue over-
Coat maybe never never O blind
With this (love) let's walk
Into the first
Rivers of morning as you are seen
To be bathed in a light white light
Come on

IN LOVE WITH YOU

1

O what a physical effect it has on me
To dive forever into the light blue sea
Of your acquaintance! Ah, but dearest friends,
Like forms, are finished, as life has ends! Still,
It is beautiful, when October
Is over, and February is over,
To sit in the starch of my shirt, and to dream of your sweet
Ways! As if the world were a taxi, you enter it, then
Reply (to no one), "Let's go five or six blocks."
Isn't the blue stream that runs past you a translation from the Russian?
Aren't my eyes bigger than love?
Isn't this history, and aren't we a couple of ruins?
Is Carthage Pompeii? is the pillow the bed? is the sun
What glues our heads together? O midnight! O midnight!
Is love what we are,
Or has happiness come to me in a private car
That's so very small I'm amazed to see it there?

2

We walk through the park in the sun, and you say, "There's a spider
Of shadow touching the bench, when morning's begun." I love you.
I love you fame I love you raining sun I love you cigarettes I love
    you love
I love you daggers I love smiles daggers and symbolism.

3

Inside the symposium of your sweetest look's
Sunflower awning by the nurse-faced chrysanthemums childhood
Again represents a summer spent sticking knives into porcelain rasp-
    berries, when China's
Still a country! Oh, King Edward abdicated years later, that's
Exactly when. If you were seventy thousand years old, and I were a
    pill,
I know I could cure your headache, like playing baseball in drinking-
    water, as baskets

Of towels sweetly touch the bathroom floor! O benches of nothing
Appear and reappear—electricity! I'd love to be how
You are, as if
The world were new, and the selves were blue
Which we don
When it's dawn,
Until evening puts on
The gray hooded selves and the light brown selves of . . .
Water! your tear-colored nail polish
Kisses me! and the lumberyard seems new
As a calm
On the sea, where, like pigeons,
I feel so mutated, sad, so breezed, so revivified, and still so unabdicated—
Not like an edge of land coming over the sea!

POEM

And so unless
I'm going to see your face
Bien soon
What's the point in everything
Going on this
Way like a chimney
Or a pint of marriage a
Western carriage
Cold and drear
Like an Afric foe
Whose stretcher bearer
Is starving while
Feeding him greens?
Yesterday you said
Today you'd say
If tomorrow has
Gone to bed (as in Proust)
Because of the rings
And the lilac weather
Of a gift;
You promised, as
The stars were
Green and blue
Points, a red and white gift; yesterday,
As I say, it was all very
Clear; and yes glitters
Upon the carriage
In green briars
And modesty, not
A baby carriage! I wish
Tears, together,
South, university, winter—
Not: jesting with
Summer, very free. I know.

I know it is white than
When hourly the grape undone
By fox's gift; and
Then too you must know
It's not really
The faculty for wishing
To stone me with paper—
Here's a kiss from today

FARM'S THOUGHTS

Hay, passion stilled the
Cool and charming disk.
Straw, I know you think I'm rude
And yet it's true: the sun's wrong.
How sweetly the weeks turned
The whole month of September.
Do I believe in you?
Does the rye believe in you?
The sunlight will last all day.
Rye, I think you are mistaken
There. Straw, kiss me. Never, hay.
The sunlight may go wrong
And create a wilderness; a wilderness
Will never create hay. Back me up, then—
The elements create a waterfall.
With vim and vigor, straw,
To avoid being stern I'll
Catapult past the green fruit
Fallen beside honor's mesh. Fresh
Green lives seem to spawn there.
The sun shines down through
Violet-besprinkled fields;
Dawn acts with a club, and we agree on everything
Long beforehand. It's the dew, hay . . .

I am the horse, alive and everything.
On the merry-go-round I made you happy as anything.
In these harvest fields they kick my body like a plaything.

I am the panther, soda fountain of the zoo;
I will represent exoticism here on the farm with you.

I am the elephant, the last laugh of hips.
I land smiling from an Africa of ships.

Near the dirt door, on the road to the farmhouse,
Please pick me up, hold me in your hands, a chicken! not a mouse,
Not a chipmunk, not a lizard, not a cow . . .

Sherbet dreams of me in winter: dairy cow.

Mother farmhouse, residual axis,
Please hear the mushroom phantom sweet
Queer clear voice of the dog-sweets
Left abandoned by a rigorous monster after . . .

Let not civilization enter! Green, draw the curtain.

Morning sweetly shines down on us pigs.
In the afternoon when the rake separates
Diet from dust, the friendly germ will separate some of us
From each other, and heads will be laid in earth.
The best thing a pig can hope for is sun.
When, shyly, in the morning, heads come forth
From the sty, we believe in everything
The air sets forth—mud, green, and trees—if the sun is shining;
If not, then it's a day like any other, a finger stuck in the earth
Like smoke, and the cold breeze of the mud, the deadly hammer
Crashing our skulls for the unreciprocating worm.

In the headlands we heard a murmur. It was the goats! We, the goats,
Wish you, Barbara and Mitchell, a happy stay on the farm.
Drink plenty of goat's milk every morning
And you will grow big and strong
Like the clouds over Mount Sinai, when Moses stood there.
We goats know our Biblical history!
Here is a red-and-blue book in which you can read
About China, and the opera in the Romance countries. Be kind
To goats, and always remember to speak in the morning
Nicely to one another, so as not to ruin the day,
Which might otherwise be spent in cursing and thrashing
As the farmer sometimes does, your Uncle Peter;
Then he kicks tin cans and pulls the beards of us goats.
It is only our love of this environment which helps us to bear
Him. We've never been anyplace else. And we send you a
Kiss.

The horses are real, Mitchell! Oh, what fun we'll have!

Get those goddamn children out of the kitchen, Uncle Lillian,
Or I'll grind them up and feed them to the pigs!

The horror of night
Descends on the cottage,
And only the goat-hair
Is visible, gleaming in the starlight.
The hay is silent. The meadow is overturned,
And the green
Where the children play
Is also the pigs' thatched cottage
Where they roost
In peace and seem
To cry past the straw and the rye to abandoned goodness,
Which is really only another word for
Feathers . . .

       Hi! Kra! Kray! Croak!
Creek! Creek! Fresh water, bleep,
Another day. Haul off and chicken
Every chicken, to chicken chicken, sorrow-pigs!

Filmed in the morning I am
A pond. Dreamed of at night I am a silver
Pond. Who's wading through me? Ugh!

I love you, hay.

I love you, straw.

And so I am the sun.
Don't you wish it about everything?

The pavement that streams past you on the wall.
My laughter is inherited from you all.
The yellow leaves and the green ones know my will.

I am the barefoot hill.

Mitchell, we'll go barefoot.

Hurry into me, the sweet day.
O leaves, can't you find another environment?
Something befriends me and hurts
At the corners of each thing I love.

It looks beautiful out.

Well, to be honest, as the color green,
I can only gather it all in once more and then let it out; this shall be
    seen
At the end of your stay. Something grows up to become a concert,
And at last the world finds him, the color grey
Accedes to red; and at the lost inn, where many pigs
Have stayed, the doorknobs when they're blue are stones;
In the midst of yellow a word may drop
Which brings it orange.

I am the color blue, on a board in the room.

Bzz, buzz, what beautiful shirttails!

Oh how through the air my beloved Master Bee sails!

GEOGRAPHY

1

In the blue hubbub of the same-through-wealth sky
Amba grew to health and fifteenth year among the jungle scrubbery.
The hate-bird sang on a lower wing of the birch-nut tree
And Amba heard him sing, and in his health he too
Began to sing, but then stopped. Along the lower Congo
There are such high plants of what there is there, when
At morning Amba heard their pink music as gentlemanly
As if he had been in civilization. When morning stank
Over the ridge of coconuts and bald fronds, with agility
Amba climbed the permanent nut trees, and will often sing
To the shining birds, and the pets in their stealth
Are each other among, also, whether it be blue (thhhh) feathers
Or green slumber. Africa in Amba's mind was those white mornings
   he sang
(thhhh) high trala to the nougat birds, and after
The trenches had all been dug for the day, Amba
Would dream at the edge of some stained and stinking pond
Of the afternight music, as blue pets came to him in his dreams;
From the orange coconuts he would extract some stained milk,
Underneath his feet roots, tangled and filthy green. At night
The moon (zzzzzz) shining down on Amba's sweet mocked sleep.

2

In Chicago Louis walked the morning's rounds with agility.
A boy of seventeen and already recognized as a fast milkman!
The whizz and burr of dead chimes oppressed the
Holocaustic unison of Frank's brain, a young outlaw
Destined to meet dishonor and truth in a same instant,
Crossing Louis' path gently in the street, the great secret unknown.

3

The fur rhubarb did not please Daisy. "Freddie," she called,
"Our fruit's gang mouldy." Daisy, white cheeks with a spot of red
In them, like apples grown in paper bags, smiled
Gently at the fresh new kitchen; and, then, depressed,
She began to cover the rhubarb with her hands.

In the crushy green ice and snow Baba ran up and around with
  exuberance!
Today, no doubt, Father and Uncle Dad would come, and together they
  three would chase the whale!
Baba stared down through the green crusty ice at the world of fish
And closed his eyes and began to imagine the sweet trip
Over the musky waters, when Daddy would spear the whale, and the
  wind
Blow "Crad, crad!" through Uncle Dad's fur, and the sweet end
Of the day where they would smile at one another over the smoking
  blubber
And Uncle Dad would tell tales of his adventures past the shadow bar
Chasing the white snow-eagle. Baba ran
Into the perfect igloo screaming with impatience, and Malmal,
His mother, kissed him and dressed him with loving care for the icy trip.

5

Ten Ko sprinted over the rice paddies. Slush, slosh, sloosh!
His brother, Wan Kai, would soon be returned from the village
Where he had gone . . . (Blue desire! . . .)

6

Roon startled her parents by appearing perfectly dressed
In a little white collar and gown.
Angebor lifted himself up so he might stare in the window at the
  pretty girl.
His little hands unclenched and dropped the coins he had saved for the
  oona.
He opened wide his eyes, then blinked at the pretty girl. He had never
  seen anything like that.
That evening, when it whitened in the sky, and a green
Clearness was there, Maggia and Angebor had no *oona*.
But Angebor talked with excitement of what he had seen, and Maggia
  drank *zee'th*.

The little prisoner wept and wailed, telling of his life in the sand
And the burning sun over the desert. And one night it was cool
And dark, and he stole away over the green sand to search for his
  parents.
And he went to their tent, and they kissed him and covered him with
  loving-kindness.
And the new morning sun shone like a pink rose in the heavens,
And the family prayed, the desert wind scorching their cool skin.

8

Amba arose. Thhhhhhh! went the birds, and clink clank cleck went
The leaves under the monkeys' feet, and Amba went to search for water
Speaking quietly with his fresh voice as he went toward Gorilla Lake
To all the beasts. Wan Kai lifted his body from the rice mat
When his brother Ten Ko came running in. "They have agreed in the
  village,"
He said. Win Tei brought them tea. Outside the rain
Fell. Plop, plop. Daisy felt something stir inside her.
She went to the window and looked out at the snow. Louis came up
  the stairs
With the milk. "Roon has bronchitis," said the American doctor,
"She will have to stay inside for ten days during this rain." Amba
Sneaked away, and wanted to go there again, but Maggia said he could
  not go again in this rain
And would be sure to lose the money for the *oona*. Baba stared
At the green and black sea. Uncle Dad stood up in the boat, while Baba
Watched Father plunge his harpoon three times in the whale. Daisy
  turned
Dreamily around, her hand on her cheek. Frank's boot
Kicked in the door. Amba wept; Ahna the deer was dead; she lay amid
  her puzzled young.
The sweet forms of the apple blossoms bent down to Wehtukai.
The boat split. Sun streamed into the apartment. Amba, Amba!
The lake was covered with gloom. Enna plunged into it screaming.

THE CIRCUS

1

We will have to go away, said the girls in the circus
And never come back any more. There is not enough of an audience
In this little town. Waiting against the black, blue sky
The big circus chariots took them into their entrances.
The light rang out over the hill where the circus wagons dimmed away.
Underneath their dresses the circus girls were sweating,
But then, an orange tight sticking to her, one spoke with
Blue eyes, she was young and pretty, blonde
With bright eyes, and she spoke with her mouth open when she sneezed
Lightly against the backs of the other girls waiting in line
To clock the rope, or come spinning down with her teeth on the line,
And she said that the circus might leave—and red posters
Stuck to the outside of the wagon, it was beginning to
Rain—she said might leave but not her heart would ever leave
Not that town but just any one where they had been, risking their lives,
And that each place they were should be celebrated by blue rosemary
In a patch, in the town. But they laughed and said Sentimental
Blonde, and she laughed, and they all, circus girls, clinging
To each other as the circus wagons rushed through the night.

2

In the next wagon, the one forward of theirs, the next wagon
Was the elephants' wagon. A grey trunk dragged on the floor . . .

3

Orville the Midget tramped up and down. Paul the Separated Man
Leaped forward. It rained and rained. Some people in the cities
Where they passed through were sitting behind thick glass
Windows, talking about their brats and drinking chocolate syrup.

4

Minnie the Rabbit fingered her machine gun.
The bright day was golden.
She aimed the immense pine needle at the foxes
Thinking Now they will never hurt my tribe any more.

The circus wagons stopped during the night
For eighteen minutes in a little town called Rosebud, Nebraska.
It was after dinner it was after bedtime it was after nausea it was
After lunchroom. The girls came out and touched each other and had
    fun
And just had time to get a breath of the fresh air of the night in
Before the ungodly procession began once more down the purple
    highway.

6

With what pomp and ceremony the circus arrived orange and red in
    the dawn!
It was exhausted, cars and wagons, and it lay down and leaped
Forward a little bit, like a fox. Minnie the Rabbit shot a little woolen
    bullet at it,
And just then the elephant man came to his doorway in the sunlight
    and stood still.

7

The snoring circus master wakes up, he takes it on himself to arrange
    the circus.
Soon the big tent floats high. Birds sing on the tent.
The parade girls and the living statue girls and the trapeze girls
Cover their sweet young bodies with phosphorescent paint.
Some of the circus girls are older women, but each is beautiful.
They stand, waiting for their cues, at the doorway of the tent.
The sky-blue lion tamer comes in, and the red giraffe manager.
They are very brave and wistful, and they look at the girls.
Some of the circus girls feel a hot sweet longing in their bodies.
But now is it time for the elephants!
Slowly the giant beasts march in. Some of their legs are clothed in
    blue papier-maché ruffles.
One has a red eye. The elephant man is at the peak of happiness.
He speaks, giddily, to every one of the circus people he passes,
He does not know what he is saying, he does not care—
His elephants are on display! They walk into the sandy ring . . .

Suddenly a great scream breaks out in the circus tent!
It is Aileen the trapeze artist, she has fallen into the dust and dirt
From so high! She must be dead! The stretcher bearers rush out,
They see her lovely human form clothed in red and white and orange
   wiry net,
And they see that she does not breathe any more.
The circus doctor leaves his tent, he runs out to care for Aileen.
He traverses the circus grounds and the dusty floor of the circus entrance,
   and he comes
Where she is, now she has begun to move again, she is not dead,
But the doctor tells her he does not know if she will ever be able to
   perform on the trapeze again,
And he sees the beautiful orange and red and white form shaken with
   sobs,
And he puts his hand on her forehead and tells her she must lie still.

9

The circus girls form a cortege, they stand in file in the yellow and
   white sunlight.
"What is death in the circus? That depends on if it is spring.
Then, if elephants are there, *mon père*, we are not completely lost.
Oh the sweet strong odor of beasts which laughs at decay!
Decay! decay! We are like the elements in a kaleidoscope,
But such passions we feel! bigger than beaches and
Rustier than harpoons." After his speech the circus practitioner sat
   down.

10

Minnie the Rabbit felt the blood leaving her little body
As she lay in the snow, orange and red and white,
A beautiful design. The dog laughs, his tongue hangs out, he looks at
   the sky.
It is white. The master comes. He laughs. He picks up Minnie the
   Rabbit
And ties her to a pine tree bough, and leaves.

11

Soon through the forest came the impassioned bumble bee.

He saw the white form on the bough. "Like rosebuds when you are thirteen," said Elmer.

Iris noticed that he didn't have any cap on.

"You must be polite when mother comes," she said.

The sky began to get grey, then the snow came.

The two tots pressed together. Elmer opened his mouth and let the snow fall in it. Iris felt warm and happy.

12

Bang! went the flyswatter. Mr. Watkins, the circus manager, looked around the room.

"Damn it, damn these flies!" he said. Mr. Loftus, the circus clerk, stared at the fly interior he had just exposed.

The circus doctor stood beside the lake. In his hand he had a black briefcase.

A wind ruffled the surface of the lake and slightly rocked the boats.

Red and green fish swam beneath the surface of the water.

The doctor went into the lunchroom and sat down. No, he said, he didn't care for anything to eat.

The soft wind of summer blew in the light green trees.

THE HISTORY OF JAZZ

The leaves of blue came drifting down.

In the corner Madeleine Reierbacher was reading *Lorna Doone*.

The bay's water helped to implement the structuring of the garden hose.

The envelope fell. Was it pink or was it red? Consult *Lorna Doone*.

There, voyager, you will find your answer. The savant grapeade stands

Remember Madeleine Reierbacher. Madeleine Reierbacher says,

"If you are happy, there is no one to keep you from being happy;

Don't let them!" Madeleine Reierbacher went into the racing car.

The racing car was orange and red. Madeleine Reierbacher drove to
Beale Street.

There Maddy doffed her garments to get into some more comfortable
clothes.

Jazz was already playing in Beale Street when Madeleine Reierbacher
arrived there.

Madeleine Reierbacher picked up the yellow horn and began to play.

No one had ever heard anything comparable to the playing of
Madeleine Reierbacher.

What a jazz musician! The pianist missed his beats because he was so
excited.

The drummer stared out the window in ecstasy at the yellow wooden trees.

The orchestra played "September in the Rain," "Mugging," and "I'm
Full of Love."

Madeleine Reierbacher rolled up her sleeves; she picked up her horn;
she played "Blues in the Rain."

It was the best jazz anyone had ever heard. It was mentioned in the
newspapers. St. Louis!

Madeleine Reierbacher became a celebrity. She played with Pesky
Summerton and Muggsy Pierce.

Madeleine cut numerous disks. Her best waxings are "Alpha Beta
and Gamma"

And "Wing Song." One day Madeleine was riding on a donkey

When she came to a yellow light; the yellow light did not change.

Madeleine kept hoping it would change to green or red. She said,
"As long as you have confidence,

You need be afraid of nothing." Madeleine saw the red smokestacks,
she looked at the thin trees,

And she regarded the railroad tracks. The yellow light was unchanging.
  Madeleine's donkey dropped dead
From his mortal load. Madeleine Reierbacher, when she fell to earth,
Picked up a blade of grass and began to play. "The Blues!" cried the
  workmen of the vicinity,
And they ran and came in great numbers to where Madeleine Reier-
  bacher was.
They saw her standing in that simple field beside the railroad track
Playing, and they saw that light changing to green and red, and they
  saw that donkey stand up
And rise into the sky; and Madeleine Reierbacher was like a clot of blue
In the midst of the blue of all that sky, and the young farmers screamed
In excitement, and the workmen dropped their heavy boards and
  stones in their excitement,
And they cried, "O Madeleine Reierbacher, play us the 'Lead Flint
  Blues' once again!"

O railroad stations, pennants, evenings, and lumberyards!
When will you ever bring us such a beautiful soloist again?
An argent strain shows on the reddish face of the sun.
Madeleine Reierbacher stands up and screams, "I am getting wet!
  You are all egotists!"
Her brain floats up into the lyric atmosphere of the sky.
We must figure out a way to keep our best musicians with us.
The finest we have always melt into the light blue sky!
In the middle of a concert, sometimes, they disappear, like anvils.
(The music comes down to us with sweet white hands on our shoulders.)
We stare up in surprise; and we hear Madeleine's best-known tune
  once again,
"If you ain't afraid of life, life can't be afraid for you."
Madeleine! Come back and sing to us!

2

Dick looked up from his blackboard.
Had he really written a history of the jazz age?
He stared at his television set; the technicolor jazz program was
  coming on.
The program that day was devoted to pictures of Madeleine Reierbacher
Playing her saxophone in the golden age of jazz.

Dick looked at his blackboard. It was a mass of green and orange lines.
Here and there a red chalk line interlaced with the others.
He stared attentively at the program.

It was a clear and blue white day. Amos said, "The calibration is
finished. Now there need be no more jazz."

In his mountain home old Lucas Dog laughed when he heard what
Amos had said.
He smilingly picked up his yellow horn to play, but all that came out
of it was steam.

COLLECTED POEMS

BUFFALO DAYS

I was asleep when you waked up the buffalo.

THE ORANGE WIVES

A mountain of funny foam went past.

GREAT HUMAN VOICES

The starlit voices drip.

COLORFUL HOUR

A few green pencils in a born pocket.

EXPRESSION

New little tray.

SLEEP

The bantam hen frayed its passage through the soft clouds.

A MINERAL WICK

Town soda.

SOMEWHERE

Between islands and envy.

CECELIA

Look, a cat.

THE SILVER WORLD

Expands.

JEWELRY SEVENTHS

Minor wonders.

AN ESKIMO COCA COLA

Three-fifths.

THE EXCEPTION PROVES THE RULE

Eight-fifths.
Nine-fifths.
Three-fifths.
Six-fifths.

THE WATER HOSE IS ON FIRE

Grapeline.

THE LINGERING MATADORS

Eskimo City.

EGYPT

Passiveness.

IS THERE A HOUSE INSIDE THAT FUEL ENGINE?

Extra aging will bring your craft over against the rosy skies.

WHY WEREN'T THEY MORE CAREFUL?

Actions.

PEANUT BUTTER CANDY

Ichthious.

THE BRINDLE COWS

Dairy farm, dairy farm,
H-O-T
H-E-A-D.

IN THE MERRY FOAM

Ask them for the blue patience of lovers.

MY MIXUP

The cherries after a shower.

MILKWEED EMBLEMS

The chambered nautilus is weak.

SUPPOSE

Red and white riding hoods.

THE GREEN MEDDLER

Aged in the fire.

A HOUSE IN MISSISSIPPI

Who stole all my new sander supplies?

WICKED OBJECTS

Aeroliths.

FRESH LIMES

A couple's bedroom slippers.

THE WINDOW

The chimney.

PAINTED FOR A ROSE

The exacting pilgrims were delighted with yellow fatigue.

NOONS

Bubbles.

ROOMS

Simplex bumblebees.

IN THE RANCHHOUSE AT DAWN

O corpuscle!
O wax town!

THE OUTSIDES OF THINGS

The sky fold, and then the bus started up.

THE BLACK LION

Never stop revealing yourself.

IN THE COAL MUD

At breakfast we could sob.

THE HAND-PAINTED EARS OF DEATH

Oh look inside me.

ALABAMA

Alabama!

PREGNANCY

Inside the pomegranate is the blue sky.

We have been living out the year in Wisconsin.
Sometimes it rains there—tremendous green drops!

We smiled up at the snow—how tremulously! Still . . .

Death is better . . .

The hog leafed through the almanac.

If there is a difference between fortune and misfortune
Which you do not catch immediately, just remember
The house of the orange and yellow squirrels, or the three pigs,
Any house which has easily distinguishable animals in it,
And remember that all animals are unfortunate.
"Yet every animal is fortunate," spoffed the mineral water
From its light green bottle on the Western tea leaves store shelf.
A bossy cow came and stood in the door;
Her hide was mangy. And then we saw the fire extinguisher. Man is
    unhappy!
A Western boy came and took the bossy cow away.
The Western boy was dressed in leather knickers, and his lean face was
    brown;
A smile played there as he looked at the sissy flowers
And led the bossy cow away to the range. In the cow's mind, pastures
    of green
Were replacing the brown architecture of the store.

Under the archways I could see the yellow pulverization
Of all you had meant to put into Paris—but they were a failure,
Your statues! your stores! and your triumphal arches!
You should have put in mere little shops selling dry goods and trumpets,
With here and there a tree and a necktie, the arch of someone's foot
Who turns out not to be beautiful, but extremely civilized, and a
    showerbath, which turns red

On certain nights, showering the green busses of my favorite city with
   cold blood! Oh ask me again
What you should do, and I will tell you differently! Ask me!

Shall any laundry be put out to dry
With so many yellow and orange sequins falling through the air?

Yes, the donkey has become very corpulent.

Will the blue carpet be sufficiently big to cover the tennis court?

Down the street walked a midget. "She's a good looker, hey?"
He said to a passer-by. O tremulous stomach!

We've been spending the winter in Paris . . .

It rains on the sweater . . .

I've a dog in my stomach!

The dogs moved delicately
On the yellow squares,
And if they sat down to play cards
Weren't they happier than we are?

I am at present owner
Of a great chain of dog-supply stores,
So naturally I hope that your child is a dog . . .

O son! or daughter!
Will you ever forgive
Your maddened daddy
For imagining a doggie
In place of a baby?

Out on the range
The blue sky is changing
To black, and the baby
Cows are rehearsing
Their lives by eating.

Near a blaze of straw
Sit the drooping cowhands;
One has on a red hat,
The other has a blue one.
They look at the babies and mothers.

Do you not think they are thinking
Thoughts like mine? O Paris,
France! with the coffee of your
Cafés, I feel life has arrived
For me! Where are you, city?

It rains on the dachshund
And the collie;
On the beach the red, green, and orange
Crustaceans are moved . . .
Tell me, sons of Atlantis, what will happen next?

THE ARTIST

Ah, well, I abandon you, cherrywood smokestack,
Near the entrance to this old green park! . . .

* * *

Cherrywood avalanche, my statue of you
Is still standing in Toledo, Ohio.
O places, summer, boredom, the static of an acrobatic blue!

And I made an amazing zinc airliner
It is standing to this day in the Minneapolis zoo . . .

Old times are not so long ago, plaster-of-paris haircut!

* * *

I often think *Play* was my best work.
It is an open field with a few boards in it.

Children are allowed to come and play in *Play*
By permission of the Cleveland Museum.
I look up at the white clouds, I wonder what I shall do, and smile.

Perhaps somebody will grow up having been influenced by *Play*,
I think—but what good will that do?
Meanwhile I am interested in steel cigarettes . . .

* * *

The orders are coming in thick and fast for steel cigarettes, steel cigars.
The Indianapolis Museum has requested six dozen packages.
I wonder if I'd still have the courage to do a thing like *Play*?

I think I may go to Cleveland . . .

* * *

Well, here I am! Pardon me, can you tell me how to get to the Cleveland
   Museum's monumental area, *Play*?

"Mister, that was torn down a long time ago. You ought to go and see
   the new thing they have now—*Gun*."
What? *Play* torn down?
"Yes, Mister, and I loved to climb in it too, when I was a kid!"
   And he shakes his head
Sadly . . . But I am thrilled beyond expectation!
He liked my work!
And I guess there must be others like that man in Cleveland too. . .

So you see, *Play* has really had its effect!
Now I am on the outskirts of town
And. . . here it is! But it has changed! There are some blue merds lying
   in the field
And it's not marked *Play* anymore—and here's a calf!
I'm so happy, I can't tell why!
Was this how I originally imagined *Play*, but lacked the courage?

It would be hard now, though, to sell it to another museum.
I wonder if the man I met's children will come and play in it?
How does one's audience survive?

*   *   *

Pittsburgh, May 16th. I have abandoned the steel cigarettes. I am
   working on *Bee*.
Bee will be a sixty-yards-long covering for the elevator shaft opening
   in the foundry sub-basement
Near my home. So far it's white sailcloth with streams of golden paint
   evenly spaced out
With a small blue pond at one end, and around it orange and green
   flowers. My experience in Cleveland affected me so
That my throat aches whenever I am not working at full speed. I have
   never been so happy and inspired and
Play seems to me now like a juvenile experience!

*   *   *

June 8th. *Bee* is still not finished. I have introduced a huge number of red balloons into it. How will it work?

Yesterday X. said, "Are you still working on *Bee*? What's happened to your interest in steel cigarettes?"

Y. said, "He hasn't been doing any work at all on them since he went to Cleveland." A shrewd guess! But how much can they possibly know?

*   *   *

November 19th. Disaster! *Bee* was almost completed, and now the immense central piece of sailcloth has torn. Impossible to repair it!

December 4th. I've gone back to work on *Bee*! I suddenly thought (after weeks of despair!), "I can place the balloons over the tear in the canvas!" So that is what I am doing. All promises to be well!

December 6th. The foreman of the foundry wants to look at my work. It seems that he too is an "artist"—does sketches and watercolors and such. . . What will he think of *Bee*?

*   *   *

Cherrywood! I had left you far from my home
And the foreman came to look at *Bee*
And the zinc airliner flew into *Play*!

The pink balloons aren't heavy, but the yellow ones break.
The foreman says, "It's the greatest thing I ever saw!"
Cleveland heard too and wants me to come back and reinaugurate *Play*

I dream of going to Cleveland but never will
Bee has obsessed my mind.

*   *   *

March 14th. A cold spring day. It is snowing. *Bee* is completed.

*   *   *

O *Bee* I think you are my best work
In the blue snow-filled air
I feel my heart break

48

I lie down in the snow
They come from the foundry and take *Bee* away
Oh what can I create now, Earth,

Green Earth on which everything blossoms anew?
"A bathroom floor cardboard trolley line
The shape and size of a lemon seed with on the inside
A passenger the size of a pomegranate seed
Who is an invalid and has to lean on the cardboard side
Of the lemon-seed-sized trolley line so that he won't fall off the train."

*   *   *

*   *   *

I just found these notes written many years ago.
How seriously I always take myself! Let it be a lesson to me.
To bring things up to date: I have just finished *Campaign*, which is
   a tremendous piece of charcoal.
Its shape is difficult to describe; but it is extremely large and would
   reach to the sixth floor of the Empire State Building. I have been
   very successful in the past fourteen or fifteen years.

*   *   *

Summer Night, shall I never succeed in finishing you? Oh you are
   the absolute end of all my creation! The ethereal beauty of that
   practically infinite number of white stone slabs stretching into the
   blue secrecy of ink! O stabs in my heart!

. . . .Why not a work *Stabs in My Heart*? But *Summer Night*?

January. . . . A troubled sleep. Can I make two things at once? What
   way is there to be sure that the impulse to work on *Stabs in My Heart* is
   serious? It seems occasioned only by my problem about finishing
   Summer Night. . . ?

*   *   *

The *Magician of Cincinnati* is now ready for human use. They are
   twenty-five tremendous stone staircases, each over six hundred feet
   high, which will be placed in the Ohio River between Cincinnati
   and Louisville, Kentucky. All the boats coming down the Ohio

49

River will presumably be smashed up against the immense statues, which are the most recent work of the creator of *Flowers*, *Bee*, *Play*, *Again* and *Human Use*. Five thousand citizens are thronged on the banks of the Ohio waiting to see the installation of the work, and the crowd is expected to be more than fifteen times its present number before morning. There will be a game of water baseball in the early afternoon, before the beginning of the ceremonies, between the Cincinnati Redlegs and the Pittsburgh Pirates. The *Magician of Cincinnati*, incidentally, is said to be absolutely impregnable to destruction of any kind, and will therefore presumably always be a feature of this part of the Ohio. . . .

*   *   *

May 16th. With what an intense joy I watched the installation of the *Magician of Cincinnati* today, in the Ohio River, where it belongs, and which is so much a part of my original scheme. . . .

May 17th. I feel suddenly freed from life—not so much as if my work were going to change, but as though I had at last seen what I had so long been prevented (perhaps I prevented myself!) from seeing: that there is too much for me to do. Somehow this enables me to relax, to breathe easily. . . .

*   *   *

There's the *Magician of Cincinnati*
In the distance
Here I am in the green trees of Pennsylvania

How strange I felt when they had installed
The *Magician*! . . . Now a bluebird trills, I am busy making my polished
    stones
For *Dresser*.

The stream the stone the birds the reddish-pink Pennsylvania hills
All go to make up *Dresser*
Why am I camping out?
I am waiting for the thousands of tons of embalming fluid
That have to come and with which I can make these hills.

*   *   *

GREATEST ARTISTIC EVENT HINTED BY GOVERNOR

Reading, June 4. Greatest artistic event was hinted today by governor. Animals converge on meadow where artist working.

CONVERGE ON MEADOW WHERE WORKING

ARTIST HINTED, SAME MAN

. . . the *Magician of Cincinnati*

THREE YEARS

October 14th. I want these hills to be striated! How naive the *Magician of Cincinnati* was! Though it makes me happy to think of it. . . . Here, I am plunged into such real earth! Striate, hills! What is this deer's head of green stone? I can't fabricate anything less than what I think should girdle the earth. . . .

PHOTOGRAPH

PHOTOGRAPH

PHOTOGRAPH

Artist who created the *Magician of Cincinnati;* Now at work in Pennsylvania; The Project—*Dresser*—So Far.

* * *

Ah! . . .

* * *

TONS

SILICON, GRASS AND DEER-HEAD RANGE

Philadelphia. Your voice as well as mine will be appreciated to express the appreciation of *Dresser*, which makes of Pennsylvania the silicon, grass and stone deer-head center of the world. . . . Artist says he may change his mind about the central bridges. Fountains to give forth real tar-water. Mountain lake in center. Real chalk cliffs. Also cliffs of clay. Deep declivities nearby. "Wanted forest atmosphere, yet to be open." Gas . . .

* * *

PHOTOGRAPH

SKETCH

DEDICATION CEREMONY

GOES SWIMMING IN OWN STREAM

SHAKING HANDS WITH GOVERNOR

COLOR PICTURE

THE HEAD OF THE ARTIST

THE ARTIST'S HAND

STACK OF ACTUAL BILLS NEEDED TO PAY FOR PROJECT

Story of *Dresser*

PENNSYLVANIA'S PRIDE: *DRESSER*

Creator of *Dresser*

* * *

STILL SMILING AT FORGE
Beverly, South Dakota, April 18. Still smiling at forge, artist of *Dresser* says, "No, of course I haven't forgotten *Dresser*. Though how quickly the years have gone by since I have been doing *Too*!" We glanced up at the sky and saw a large white bird, somewhat similar to an immense seagull, which was as if fixed above our heads. Its eyes were blue sapphires, and its wings were formed by an ingenious arrangement of whitened daffodil-blossom parts. Its body seemed mainly charcoal, on the whole, with a good deal of sand mixed in. As we watched it, the creature actually seemed to move. . . .

August 4th . . . Three four five, and it's finished! I can see it in Beverly . . .

*   *   *

BEVERLY HONORS ARTIST. CALLED "FOUNDING FATHER"

Beverly, South Dakota, August 14 . . .

MISSISSIPPI CLAIMS BIRTHPLACE

HONORS BIRTHPLACE

BIRTHPLACE HONORS HELD

*   *   *

INDIANS AND SAVANTS MEET TO PRAISE *WEST WIND*

PAT HONORED

PAT AND *WEST WIND* HONORED

*   *   *

June 3rd. It doesn't seem possible—the Pacific Ocean! I have ordered sixteen million tons of blue paint. Waiting anxiously for it to arrive. How would grass be as a substitute? cement?

*   *   *

FRESH AIR

1

At the Poem Society a black-haired man stands up to say
"You make me sick with all your talk about restraint and mature talent!
Haven't you ever looked out the window at a painting by Matisse,
Or did you always stay in hotels where there were too many spiders
    crawling on your visages?
Did you ever glance inside a bottle of sparkling pop,
Or see a citizen split in two by the lightning?
I am afraid you have never smiled at the hibernation
Of bear cubs except that you saw in it some deep relation
To human suffering and wishes, oh what a bunch of crackpots!"
The black-haired man sits down, and the others shoot arrows at him.
A blond man stands up and says,
"He is right! Why should we be organized to defend the kingdom
Of dullness? There are so many slimy people connected with poetry,
Too, and people who know nothing about it!
I am not recommending that poets like each other and organize to fight
    them,
But simply that lightning should strike them."
Then the assembled mediocrities shot arrows at the blond-haired man.
The chairman stood up on the platform, oh he was physically ugly!
He was small-limbed and -boned and thought he was quite seductive,
But he was bald with certain hideous black hairs,
And his voice had the sound of water leaving a vaseline bathtub,
And he said, "The subject for this evening's discussion is poetry
On the subject of love between swans." And everyone threw candy
    hearts
At the disgusting man, and they stuck to his bib and tucker,
And he danced up and down on the platform in terrific glee
And recited the poetry of his little friends—but the blond man stuck
    his head
Out of a cloud and recited poems about the east and thunder,
And the black-haired man moved through the stratosphere chanting
Poems of the relationships between terrific prehistoric charcoal whales,
And the slimy man with candy hearts sticking all over him
Wilted away like a cigarette paper on which the bumblebees have
    urinated,
And all the professors left the room to go back to their duty,

And all that were left in the room were five or six poets
And together they sang the new poem of the twentieth century
Which, though influenced by Mallarmé, Shelley, Byron, and Whitman,
Plus a million other poets, is still entirely original
And is so exciting that it cannot be here repeated.
You must go to the Poem Society and wait for it to happen.
Once you have heard this poem you will not love any other,
Once you have dreamed this dream you will be inconsolable,
Once you have loved this dream you will be as one dead,
Once you have visited the passages of this time's great art!

2

"Oh to be seventeen years old
Once again," sang the red-haired man, "and not know that poetry
Is ruled with the sceptre of the dumb, the deaf, and the creepy!"
And the shouting persons battered his immortal body with stones
And threw his primitive comedy into the sea
From which it sang forth poems irrevocably blue.

Who are the great poets of our time, and what are their names?
Yeats of the baleful influence, Auden of the baleful influence, Eliot of
    the baleful influence
(Is Eliot a great poet? no one knows), Hardy, Stevens, Williams (is
    Hardy of our time?),
Hopkins (is Hopkins of our time?), Rilke (is Rilke of our time?), Lorca
    (is Lorca of our time?), who is still of our time?
Mallarmé, Valéry, Apollinaire, Eluard, Reverdy, French poets are
    still of our time,
Pasternak and Mayakovsky, is Jouve of our time?

Where are young poets in America, they are trembling in publishing
    houses and universities,
Above all they are trembling in universities, they are bathing the
    library steps with their spit,
They are gargling out innocuous (to whom?) poems about maple trees
    and their children,
Sometimes they brave a subject like the Villa d'Este or a lighthouse in
    Rhode Island,
Oh what worms they are! they wish to perfect their form.

Yet could not these young men, put in another profession,
Succeed admirably, say at sailing a ship? I do not doubt it, Sir, and
I wish we could try them.
(A plane flies over the ship holding a bomb but perhaps it will not
drop the bomb,
The young poets'from the universities are staring anxiously at the skies,
Oh they are remembering their days on the campus when they looked
up to watch birds excrete,
They are remembering the days they spent making their elegant poems.)

Is there no voice to cry out from the wind and say what it is like to be
the wind,
To be roughed up by the trees and to bring music from the scattered
houses
And the stones, and to be in such intimate relationship with the sea
That you cannot understand it? Is there no one who feels like a pair
of pants?

3

Summer in the trees! "It is time to strangle several bad poets."
The yellow hobbyhorse rocks to and fro, and from the chimney
Drops the Strangler! The white and pink roses are slightly agitated
by the struggle,
But afterwards beside the dead "poet" they cuddle up comfortingly
against their vase. They are safer now, no one will compare them to
the sea.

Here on the railroad train, one more time, is the Strangler.
He is going to get that one there, who is on his way to a poetry reading.
Agh! Biff! A body falls to the moving floor.

In the football stadium I also see him,
He leaps through the frosty air at the maker of comparisons
Between football and life and silently, silently strangles him!

Here is the Strangler dressed in a cowboy suit
Leaping from his horse to annihilate the students of myth!

The Strangler's ear is alert for the names of Orpheus,
Cuchulain, Gawain, and Odysseus,
And for poems addressed to Jane Austen, F. Scott Fitzgerald,
To Ezra Pound, and to personages no longer living
Even in anyone's thoughts—O Strangler the Strangler!

He lies on his back in the waves of the Pacific Ocean.

4

Supposing that one walks out into the air
On a fresh spring day and has the misfortune
To encounter an article on modern poetry
In *New World Writing*, or has the misfortune
To see some examples of some of the poetry
Written by the men with their eyes on the myth
And the Missus and the midterms, in the *Hudson Review*,
Or, if one is abroad, in *Botteghe Oscure*,
Or indeed in *Encounter*, what is one to do
With the rest of one's day that lies blasted to ruins
All bluely about one, what is one to do?
O surely one cannot complain to the President,
Nor even to the deans of Columbia College,
Nor to T. S. Eliot, nor to Ezra Pound,
And supposing one writes to the Princess Caetani,
"Your poets are awful!" what good would it do?
And supposing one goes to the *Hudson Review*
With a package of matches and sets fire to the building?
One ends up in prison with trial subscriptions
To the *Partisan*, *Sewanee*, and *Kenyon Review*!

5

Sun out! perhaps there is a reason for the lack of poetry
In these ill-contented souls, perhaps they need air!

Blue air, fresh air, come in, I welcome you, you are an art student,
Take off your cap and gown and sit down on the chair.
Together we shall paint the poets—but no, air! perhaps you should
  go to them, quickly,
Give them a little inspiration, they need it, perhaps they are out of
  breath,

Give them a little inhuman company before they freeze the English language to death!

(And rust their typewriters a little, be sea air! be noxious! kill them, if you must, but stop their poetry!

I remember I saw you dancing on the surf on the Côte d'Azur,

And I stopped, taking my hat off, but you did not remember me,

Then afterwards you came to my room bearing a handful of orange flowers

And we were together all through the summer night!)

That we might go away together, it is so beautiful on the sea, there are a few white clouds in the sky!

But no, air! you must go . . . Ah, stay!

But she has departed and . . . Ugh! what poisonous fumes and clouds! what a suffocating atmosphere!

Cough! whose are these hideous faces I see, what is this rigor

Infecting the mind? where are the green Azores,

Fond memories of childhood, and the pleasant orange trolleys,

A girl's face, red-white, and her breasts and calves, blue eyes, brown eyes, green eyes, fahrenheit

Temperatures, dandelions, and trains, O blue?!

Wind, wind, what is happening? Wind! I can't see any bird but the gull, and I feel it should symbolize . . .

Oh, pardon me, there's a swan, one two three swans, a great white swan, hahaha how pretty they are! Smack!

Oh! stop! help! yes, I see—disrespect of my superiors—forgive me, dear Zeus, nice Zeus, parabolic bird, O feathered excellence! white!

There is Achilles too, and there's Ulysses, I've always wanted to see them, hahaha!

And there is Helen of Troy, I suppose she is Zeus too, she's so terribly pretty—hello, Zeus, my you are beautiful, Bang!

One more mistake and I get thrown out of the Modern Poetry Association, help! Why aren't there any adjectives around?

Oh there are, there's practically nothing else—look, here's *grey*, *utter*, *agonized*, *total*, *phenomenal*, *gracile*, *invidious*, *sundered*, and *fused*,

Elegant, *absolute*, *pyramidal*, and . . . Scream! but what can I describe with these words? States!

States symbolized and divided by two, complex states, magic states, states of consciousness governed by an aroused sincerity, cockadoodle doo!

Another bird! is it morning? Help! where am I? am I in the barnyard? oink oink, scratch, moo! Splash!

My first lesson. "Look around you. What do you think and feel?" *Uhhh* . . . "Quickly!" *This Connecticut landscape would have pleased Vermeer.* Wham! A-Plus. "Congratulations!" I am promoted.

OOOhhhhh I wish I were dead, what a headache! My second lesson: "Rewrite your first lesson line six hundred times. Try to make it into a magnetic field." I can do it too. But my poor line! What a nightmare! Here comes a tremendous horse,

Trojan, I presume. No, it's my third lesson. "Look, look! Watch him, see what he's doing? That's what we want you to do. Of course it won't be the same as his at first, but . . ." I demur. Is there no other way to fertilize minds?

Bang! I give in . . . Already I see my name in two or three anthologies, a serving girl comes into the barn bringing me the anthologies,

She is very pretty and I smile at her a little sadly, perhaps it is my last smile! Perhaps she will hit me! But no, she smiles in return, and she takes my hand.

My hand, my hand! what is this strange thing I feel in my hand, on my arm, on my chest, my face—can it be . . .? it is! AIR!

Air, air, you've come back! Did you have any success? "What do you think?" I don't know, air. You are so strong, air.

And she breaks my chains of straw, and we walk down the road, behind us the hideous fumes!

Soon we reach the seaside, she is a young art student who places her head on my shoulder,

I kiss her warm red lips, and here is the Strangler, reading the *Kenyon Review*! Good luck to you, Strangler!

Goodbye, Helen! goodbye, fumes! goodbye, abstracted dried-up boys! goodbye, dead trees! goodbye, skunks!

Goodbye, manure! goodbye, critical manicure! goodbye, you big fat men standing on the east coast as well as the west giving poems the test! farewell, Valéry's stern dictum!

Until tomorrow, then, scum floating on the surface of poetry! goodbye for a moment, refuse that happens to land in poetry's boundaries! adieu, stale eggs teaching imbeciles poetry to bolster up your egos! adios, boring anomalies of these same stale eggs!

Ah, but the scum is deep! Come, let me help you! and soon we pass into the clear blue water. Oh GOODBYE, castrati of poetry! farewell, stale pale skunky pentameters (the only honest English meter, gloop gloop!) until tomorrow, horrors! oh, farewell!

Hello, sea! good morning, sea! hello, clarity and excitement, you great expanse of green—

O green, beneath which all of them shall drown!

THANKSGIVING

What's sweeter than at the end of a summer's day
To suddenly drift away
From the green match-wrappers in an opened pocketbook
And be part of the boards in a tavern?

A tavern made of new wood.
There's an orange-red sun in the sky
And a redskin is hunting for you underneath ladders of timber.
I will buy this tavern. Will you buy this tavern? I do.

In the Indian camp there's awful dismay.
Do they know us as we know they
Know us or will know us, I mean a—
I mean a hostile force, the month of May.

How whitely the springtime is blossoming,
Ugh! all around us!
It is the brilliant Indian time of year
When the sweetest Indians mate with the sweetest others.

But I fear the white men, I fear
The rent apple blossoms and discarded feathers
And the scalp lying secretly on the ground
Like an unoffending nose!

But we've destroyed all that. With shocking guns.
Peter Stuyvesant, Johnny Appleseed,
We've destroyed all that. Come,
Do you believe right was on either side?

How would you like to be living in an Indian America,
With feathers dressing every head? We'd eat buffalo hump
For Thanksgiving dinner. Everyone is in a tribe.
A girl from the Bep Tribe can't marry a brave from the Bap Tribe.
    Is that democracy?

And then those dreary evenings around the campfires
Listening to the Chief! If there were a New York
It would be a city of tents, and what do you suppose
Our art and poetry would be like? For the community! the tribe!
No beautiful modern abstract pictures, no mad incomprehensible
Free lovable poems! And our moral sense! tribal.
If you would like to be living in an Indian America
Why not subscribe to this newspaper, *Indian America*?

In Wisconsin, Ben, I stand, I walk up and down and try to decide.

Is this country getting any better or has it gotten?
If the Indian New York is bad, what about our white New York?
Dirty, unwholesome, the filthy appendage to a vast ammunition works,
    I hate it!
Disgusting rectangular garbage dump sending its fumes up to suffocate
    the sky—
Foo, what fumes! and the scaly white complexion of her citizens.
There's hell in every firm handshake, and stifled rage in every look.
If you do find somewhere to lie down, it's a dirty inspected corner,
And there are newspapers and forums and the stinking breath of
    Broadway
To investigate what it feels like to be a source of stench
And nothing else. And if one does go away,
It is always here, waiting, for one to come back. And one does come
    back,
As one comes back to the bathroom, and to a time of suffering.

Where else would I find such ardent and graceful spirits
Inspired and wasted and using and used by this horrible city,
New York, New York? Can the Pilgrims' Thanksgiving dinner really
    compare to it?
And the Puritans? And the single-minded ankle-divided Indians?
No, nothing can compare to it! So it's here we speak from the heart,
And it's rotting so fast that what we say
Fades like the last of a summer's day,
Rot which makes us prolific as the sun on white unfastened clouds.

PERMANENTLY

One day the Nouns were clustered in the street.
An Adjective walked by, with her dark beauty.
The Nouns were struck, moved, changed.
The next day a Verb drove up, and created the Sentence.

Each Sentence says one thing—for example, "Although it was a dark
   rainy day when the Adjective walked by, I shall remember the pure
   and sweet expression on her face until the day I perish from the green,
   effective earth."
Or, "Will you please close the window, Andrew?"
Or, for example, "Thank you, the pink pot of flowers on the window
   sill has changed color recently to a light yellow, due to the heat from
   the boiler factory which exists nearby."

In the springtime the Sentences and the Nouns lay silently on the grass.
A lonely Conjunction here and there would call, "And! But!"
But the Adjective did not emerge.

As the adjective is lost in the sentence,
So I am lost in your eyes, ears, nose, and throat—
You have enchanted me with a single kiss
Which can never be undone
Until the destruction of language.

DOWN AT THE DOCKS

Down at the docks
Where everything is sweet and inclines
At night
To the sound of canoes
I planted a maple tree
And every night
Beneath it I studied the cosmos
Down at the docks.

Sweet ladies, listen to me.
The dock is made of wood
The maple tree's not made of wood
It is wood
Wood comes from it
As music comes from me
And from this mandolin I've made
Out of the maple tree.

Jealous gentlemen, study how
Wood comes from the maple
Then devise your love
So that it seems
To come from where
All is it yet something more
White spring flowers and leafy bough
Jealous gentlemen.

Arrogant little waves
Knocking at the dock
It's for you I've made this chanson
For you and that big dark blue.

YOU WERE WEARING

You were wearing your Edgar Allan Poe printed cotton blouse.

In each divided up square of the blouse was a picture of Edgar Allan Poe.

Your hair was blonde and you were cute. You asked me, "Do most boys think that most girls are bad?"

I smelled the mould of your seaside resort hotel bedroom on your hair held in place by a John Greenleaf Whittier clip.

"No," I said, "it's girls who think that boys are bad." Then we read *Snowbound* together

And ran around in an attic, so that a little of the blue enamel was scraped off my George Washington, Father of His Country, shoes.

Mother was walking in the living room, her Strauss Waltzes comb in her hair.

We waited for a time and then joined her, only to be served tea in cups painted with pictures of Herman Melville

As well as with illustrations from his book *Moby Dick* and from his novella, *Benito Cereno*.

Father came in wearing his Dick Tracy necktie: "How about a drink, everyone?"

I said, "Let's go outside a while." Then we went onto the porch and sat on the Abraham Lincoln swing.

You sat on the eyes, mouth, and beard part, and I sat on the knees.

In the yard across the street we saw a snowman holding a garbage can lid smashed into a likeness of the mad English king, George the Third.

LOCKS

These locks on doors have brought me happiness:
The lock on the door of the sewing machine in the living room
Of a tiny hut in which I was living with a mad seamstress;
The lock on the filling station one night when I was drunk
And had the idea of enjoying a nip of petroleum;
The lock on the family of seals, which, when released, would have bitten;
The lock on the life raft when I was taking a bath instead of drowning;
The lock inside the nose of the contemporary composer who was playing
    the piano and would have ruined his concert by sneezing, while I
    was turning pages;
The lock on the second hump of a camel while I was not running out
    of water in the desert;
The lock on the fish hatchery the night we came up from the beach
And were trying to find a place to spend the night—it was full of
    contagious fish;
The lock on my new necktie when I was walking through a stiff wind
On my way to an appointment at which I had to look neat and simple;
The lock on the foghorn the night of the lipstick parade—
If the foghorn had sounded, everyone would have run inside before
    the most beautiful contestant appeared;
The lock in my hat when I saw her and which kept me from tipping it,
Which she would not have liked, because she believed that naturalness
    was the most friendly;
The lock on the city in which we would not have met anyone we knew;
The lock on the airplane which was flying without a pilot
Above Miami Beach on the night when I unlocked my bones
To the wind, and let the gales of sweetness blow through me till
    I shuddered and shook
Like a key in a freezing hand, and ran up into the Miami night air
    like a stone;
The lock on the hayfield, which kept me from getting out of bed
To meet the hayfield committee there; the lock on the barn, that
    kept the piled-up hay away from me;

The lock on the mailboat that kept it from becoming a raincoat
On the night of the thunderstorm; the lock on the sailboat
That keeps it from taking me away from you when I am asleep with you,
And, when I am not, the lock on my sleep, that keeps me from waking
  and finding you are not there.

VARIATIONS ON A THEME BY WILLIAM CARLOS WILLIAMS

1

I chopped down the house that you had been saving to live in next
    summer.
I am sorry, but it was morning, and I had nothing to do
and its wooden beams were so inviting.

2

We laughed at the hollyhocks together
and then I sprayed them with lye.
Forgive me. I simply do not know what I am doing.

3

I gave away the money that you had been saving to live on for the
    next ten years.
The man who asked for it was shabby
and the firm March wind on the porch was so juicy and cold.

4

Last evening we went dancing and I broke your leg.
Forgive me. I was clumsy, and
I wanted you here in the wards, where I am the doctor!

THANK YOU

Oh thank you for giving me the chance
Of being ship's doctor! I am sorry that I shall have to refuse—
But, you see, the most I know of medicine is orange flowers
Tilted in the evening light against a cashmere red
Inside which breasts invent the laws of light
And of night, where cashmere moors itself across the sea.
And thank you for giving me these quintuplets
To rear and make happy . . . My mind was on something else.

Thank you for giving me this battleship to wash,
But I have a rash on my hands and my eyes hurt,
And I know so little about cleaning a ship
That I should rather clean an island.
There one knows what one is about—sponge those palm trees, sweep
   up the sand a little, polish those coconuts;
Then take a rest for a while and it's time to trim the grass as well as
   separate it from each other where gummy substances have made
   individual blades stick together, forming an ugly bunch;
And then take the dead bark off the trees, and perfume these islands
   a bit with a song. . . . That's easy—but a battleship!
Where does one begin and how does one do? to batten the hatches?
   I would rather clean a million palm trees.

Now here comes an offer of a job for setting up a levee
In Mississippi. No thanks. Here it says *Rape or Worse*. I think they
   must want me to publicize this book.
On the jacket it says "Published in Boothbay Harbor, Maine"—what
   a funny place to publish a book!
I suppose it is some provincial publishing house
Whose provincial pages emit the odor of sails
And the freshness of the sea
Breeze. . . . But publicity!

The only thing I could publicize well would be my tooth,
Which I could say came with my mouth and in a most engaging manner
With my whole self, my body and including my mind,
Spirits, emotions, spiritual essences, emotional substances, poetry,
    dreams, and lords
Of my life, everything, all embraceleted with my tooth
In a way that makes one wish to open the windows and scream "Hi!"
    to the heavens,
And "Oh, come and take me away before I die in a minute!"

It is possible that the dentist is smiling, that he dreams of extraction
Because he believes that the physical tooth and the spiritual tooth are
    one.

Here is another letter, this one from a textbook advertiser;
He wants me to advertise a book on chopping down trees.
But how could I? I love trees! and I haven't the slightest sympathy
    with chopping them down, even though I know
We need their products for wood-fires, some houses, and maple syrup—
Still I like trees better
In their standing condition, when they sway at the beginning of
    evening . . .
And thank you for the pile of driftwood.
Am I wanted at the sea?

And thank you for the chance to run a small hotel
In an elephant stopover in Zambezi,
But I do not know how to take care of guests, certainly they would all
    leave soon
After seeing blue lights out the windows and rust on their iron beds—
    I'd rather own a bird-house in Jamaica:
Those people come in, the birds, they do not care how things are kept
    up . . .
It's true that Zambezi proprietorship would be exciting, with people
    getting off elephants and coming into my hotel,
But as tempting as it is I cannot agree.
And thank you for this offer of the post of referee
For the Danish wrestling championship—I simply do not feel
    qualified . . .

But the fresh spring air has been swabbing my mental decks
Until, although prepared for fight, still I sleep on land.
Thank you for the ostriches. I have not yet had time to pluck them,
But I am sure they will be delicious, adorning my plate at sunset,
My tremendous plate, and the plate
Of the offers to all my days. But I cannot fasten my exhilaration to
  the sun.

And thank you for the evening of the night on which I fell off my horse
  in the shadows. That was really useful.

LUNCH

The lanternslides grinding out B-flat minor
Chords to the ears of the deaf youngster who sprays in Hicksville
The sides of a car with the dream-splitting paint
Of pianos (he dreamt of one day cutting the Conservatory
In two with his talent), these lanternslides, I say,
They are— The old woman hesitated. A lifesaver was shoved down
  her throat; then she continued:
They are some very good lanternslides in that bunch. Then she
  fainted
And we revived her with flowers. She smiled sleepily at the sun.
He is my own boy, she said, with her glass hand falling through the
  sparkling red America of lunch.

That old boilermaker she has in her back yard,
Olaf said, used to be her sweetheart years back.
One day, though, a train passed, and pressed her hard,
And she deserted life and love for liberty.
We carried Olaf softly into the back yard
And laid him down with his head under the steamroller.
Then Jill took the wheel and I tinkered with the engine,
Till we rolled him under, rolled him under the earth.
When people ask us what's in our back yard
Now, we don't like to tell them, Jill says, laying her silver bandannaed
  head on my greened bronze shoulder.
Then we both dazzle ourselves with the red whiteness of lunch.

That old woman named Tessie Runn
Had a tramp boyfriend who toasted a bun.
They went to Florida, but Maxine Schweitzer was hard of
Hearing and the day afterwards the judge adjourned the trial.
When it finally came for judgment to come up
Of delicious courtyards near the Pantheon,
At last we had to let them speak, the children whom flowers had made
  statues
For the rivers of water which came from their funnel;
And we stood there in the middle of existence
Dazzled by the white paraffin of lunch.

Music in Paris and water coming out from the flannel
Of the purist person galloping down the Madeleine
Toward a certain wafer. Hey! just a minute! the sunlight is being
    rifled
By the green architecture of the flowers. But the boulevard turned a
    big blue deaf ear
Of cinema placards to the detonated traveler. He had forgotten the
    blue defilade of lunch!

Genoa! a stone's throw from Acapulco
If an engine were built strong enough,
And down where the hulls and scungilli,
Glisteningly unconscious, agree,
I throw a game of shoes with Horace Sturnbul
And forget to eat lunch.

O launch, lunch, you dazzling hoary tunnel
To paradise!
Do you see that snowman tackled over there
By summer and the sea? A boardwalk went to Istanbul
And back under his left eye. We saw the Moslems praying
In Rhodes. One had a red fez, another had a black cap.
And in the extended heat of afternoon,
As an ice-cold gradual sweat covered my whole body,
I realized, and the carpet swam like a red world at my feet
In which nothing was green, and the Moslems went on praying,
That we had missed lunch, and a perpetual torrent roared into the sea
Of my understanding. An old woman gave us bread and rolls on the
    street.

The dancing wagon has come! here is the dancing wagon!
Come up and get lessons—here is lemonade and grammar!
Here is drugstore and cowboy—all that is America—plus sex, perfumes,
    and shimmers—all the Old World;
Come and get it—and here is your reading matter
For twenty-nine centuries, and here finally is lunch—
To be served in the green defilade under the roaring tower
Where Portugal meets Spain inside a flowered madeleine.

My ginger dress has nothing on, but yours
Has on a picture of Queen Anne Boleyn
Surrounded by her courtiers eating lunch
And on the back a one of Henry the Eighth
Summoning all his courtiers in for lunch.

And the lunchboat has arrived
From Spain.
Everyone getting sick is on it;
The bold people and the sadists are on it;
I am glad I am not on it,
I am having a big claw of garlic for lunch—
But it plucks me up in the air,
And there, above the ship, on a cloud
I see the angels eating lunch.
One has a beard, another a moustache,
And one has some mustard smeared on his ears.
A couple of them ask me if I want to go to Honolulu,
And I accept—it's all right—
Another time zone: we'll be able to have lunch.
They are very beautiful and transparent,
My two traveling companions,
And they will go very well with Hawaii
I realize as we land there,
That dazzling red whiteness—it is our desire . . .
For whom? The angels of lunch.

Oh I sat over a glass of red wine
And you came out dressed in a paper cup.
An ant-fly was eating hay-mire in the chair-rafters
And large white birds flew in and dropped edible animals to the ground.
If they had been gulls it would have been garbage
Or fish. We have to be fair to the animal kingdom,
But if I do not wish to be fair, if I wish to eat lunch
Undisturbed—? The light of day shines down. The world continues.

We stood in the little hutment in Biarritz
Waiting for lunch, and your hand clasped mine
And I felt it was sweaty;
And then lunch was served,
Like the bouquet of an enchantress.
Oh the green whites and red yellows
And purple whites of lunch!

The bachelor eats his lunch,
The married man eats his lunch,
And old Uncle Joris belches
The seascape in which a child appears
Eating a watermelon and holding a straw hat.
He moves his lips as if to speak
But only sea air emanates from this childish beak.
It is the moment of sorrows,
And in the shores of history,
Which stretch in both directions, there are no happy tomorrows.
But Uncle Joris holds his apple up and begins to speak
To the child. Red waves fan my universe with the green macaw of
    lunch.

This street is deserted;
I think my eyes are empty;
Let us leave
Quickly.
Day bangs on the door and is gone.

Then they picked him up and carried him away from that company.
When he awoke he was in the fire department, and sleepy but not tired.
They gave him a hoseful of blue Spain to eat for lunch,
And Portugal was waiting for him at the door, like a rainstorm of
    evening raspberries.

It is time to give lunch to my throat and not my chest.
What? either the sting ray has eaten my lunch
Or else—and she searches the sky for something else; ·
But I am far away, seeming blue-eyed, empirical . . .

Let us give lunch to the lunch—
But how shall we do it?
The headwaiters expand and confer;
Will little pieces of cardboard box do it?
And what about silver and gold pellets?
The headwaiters expand and confer:
And what if the lunch should refuse to eat anything at all?
Why then we'd say be damned to it,
And the red doorway would open on a green railway
And the lunch would be put in a blue car
And it would go away to Whippoorwill Valley
Where it would meet and marry Samuel Dogfoot, and bring forth seven
    offspring,
All of whom would be half human, half lunch;
And when we saw them, sometimes, in the gloaming,
We would take off our mining hats and whistle Tweet twee-oo,
With watering mouths staring at the girls in pink organdy frocks,
Not realizing they really were half edible,
And we would die still without knowing it;
So to prevent anything happening that terrible
Let's give everybody we see and like a good hard bite right now,
To see what they are, because it's time for lunch!

TAKING A WALK WITH YOU

My misunderstandings: for years I thought "muso bello" meant
    "Bell Muse," I thought it was a kind of
Extra reward on the slotmachine of my shyness in the snow when
February was only a bouncing ball before the Hospital of the
    Two Sisters of the Last
Hamburger Before I Go to Sleep. I thought Axel's Castle
    was a garage;
And I had beautiful dreams about it, too—sensual, mysterious
    mechanisms; horns honking, wheels turning . . .
My misunderstandings were:
1)   thinking Pinocchio could really change from a puppet into a
    real boy, and back again!
2)   thinking it depended on whether he was good or bad!
3)   identifying him with myself!
4)   and therefore every time I was bad being afraid I would turn
    into wood . . .
5)   I misunderstood childhood. I usually liked the age I was.
    However, now I regard twenty-nine as an optimum age (for me).
6)   I disliked Shelley between twenty and twenty-five.
All of these things I suppose are understandable, but
When you were wearing your bodice I did not understand that you
    had nothing on beneath it;
When my father turned the corner I misunderstood the light very much
On Fifty-fifth Street; and I misunderstood (like an old Chinese
    restaurant) what he was doing there.
I misunderstand generally Oklahoma and Arkansas, though I think I
    understand New Mexico;
I understand the Painted Desert, cowboy hats, and vast spaces; I do
Not understand hillbilly life—I am sure I misunderstand it.
I did not understand that you had nothing on beneath your bodice
Nor, had I understood this, would I have understood what it meant;
    even now I
(Merry Christmas! Here, Father, take your package) misunderstand it!
Merry Christmas, Uncle Leon! yes, here is your package too.

I misunderstand Renaissance life; I misunderstand:
The Renaissance;
Ancient China;

The Middle Atlantic States and what they are like;
The tubes of London and what they mean;
Titian, Michelangelo, Vermeer;
The origins of words;
What others are talking about;
Music from the beginnings to the present time;
Laughter; and tears, even more so;
Value (economic and esthetic);
Snow (and weather in the country);
The meaning of the symbols and myths of Christmas.
I misunderstand you,
I misunderstand the day we walked down the street together for ten
    hours—
Where were we going? I had thought we were going somewhere. I
    believe I misunderstand many of the places we passed and things
    you said . . .
I misunderstand "Sons of Burgundy,"
I misunderstand that you had nothing painted beneath your bodice,
I misunderstand "Notification of Arrival or Departure to Be Eradicated
    Before Affection of Deceased Tenant."
I understand that
The smoke and the clouds are both a part of the day, but

I misunderstand the words "After Departure,"
I misunderstand nothingness;
I misunderstand the attitude of people in pharmacies, on the decks of
    ships, in my bedroom, amid the pine needles, on mountains of
    cotton, everywhere—
When they say paralytic I hear parasite, and when they say coffee I
    think music . . .
What is wrong with me from head to toe
That I misinterpret everything I hear? I misunderstand:
French: often;
Italian: sometimes, almost always—for example, if someone says,
    "Fortunate ones!" I am likely to think he is referring to the fountain
    with blue and red water (I am likely to make this mistake also in
    English).
I misunderstand Greek entirely;
I find ancient Greece very hard to understand: I probably misunder-
    stand it;

I misunderstand spoken German about 98% of the time, like the
   cathedral in the middle of a town;
I misunderstand "Beautiful Adventures"; I also think I probably
   misunderstand *La Nausée* by Jean-Paul Sartre . . .
I probably misunderstand misunderstanding itself—I misunderstand
   the Via Margutta in Rome, or Via della Vite, no matter what
   street, all of them.
I misunderstand wood in the sense of its relationship to the tree; I
   misunderstand people who take one attitude or another about it . . .
Spring I would like to say I understand, but I most probably don't—
   autumn, winter, and summer are all in the same boat
(Ruined ancient cities by the sea).

I misunderstand *vacation* and *umbrella*,
I misunderstand *motion* and *weekly*
(Though I think I understand "Daytime Pissarros"
And the octagon—I do not understand the public garden) . . .

Oh I am sure there is a use for all of them, but what is it?
My misunderstandings confuse Rome and Ireland, and can you
Bring that beautiful sex to bear upon it?
I misunderstand what I am saying, though not to you;
I misunderstand a large boat: that is a ship.
What you are feeling for me I misunderstand totally; I think I mis-
   understand the very possibilities of feeling,
Especially here in Rome, where I somehow think I am.
I see the sky, and sails.
(I misunderstand the mustard and the bottle)
Oh that we could go sailing in that sky!

What tune came with the refreshments?
I am unable to comprehend why they were playing off key.
Is it because they wanted us to jump over the cliff
Or was one of them a bad or untrained musician
Or the whole lot of them?
At any rate
San Giovanni in Laterano
Also resisted my questioning
And turned a deaf blue dome to me
Far too successfully.

I cannot understand why you walk forwards and backwards with me.
I think it is because you want to try out your shoes for their toes.
It is Causation that is my greatest problem
And after that the really attentive study of millions of details.

I love you, but it is difficult to stop writing.
As a flea could write the Divine Comedy of a water jug. Now Irish
    mists close in upon us.
Peat sails through the air, and greenness becomes bright. Are you the
    ocean or the island? Am I on Irish soil, or are your waves covering
    me?
St. Peter's bells are ringing: "Earthquake, inundation, and sleep to the
    understanding!"
(American Express! flower vendors! your beautiful straight nose!
    that delightful trattoria in Santa Maria in Trastevere!)
Let us have supper at Santa Maria in Trastevere
Where by an absolute and total misunderstanding (but not fatal) I
    once ate before I met you.
I am probably misinterpreting your answer, since I hear nothing, and
    I believe I am alone.

THE RAILWAY STATIONERY

The railway stationery lay upon
The desk of the railway clerk, from where he could see
The springtime and the tracks. Engraved upon
Each page was an inch-and-a-half-high T
And after that an H and then an E
And then, slightly below it to the right,
There was COLUMBUS RAILWAY COMPANY
In darker ink as the above was light.
The print was blue. And just beneath it all
There was an etching—not in blue, but black—
Of a real railway engine half-an-inch tall
Which, if you turned the paper on its back,
You could see showing through, as if it ran
To one edge of the sheet then back again.

To one edge of the sheet then back again!
The springtime comes while we're still drenched in snow
And, whistling now, snow-spotted Number Ten
Comes up the track and stops, and we must go
Outside to get its cargo, with our hands
Cold as the steel they touch. Inside once more
Once we have shut the splintery wooden door
Of the railway shack, the stationery demands
Some further notice. For the first time the light,
Reflected from the snow by the bright spring sun,
Shows that the engine wheel upon the right
Is slightly darker than the left-side one
And slightly lighter than the one in the center,
Which may have been an error of the printer.

Shuffling through many sheets of it to establish
Whether this difference is consistent will
Prove that it is not. Probably over-lavish
At the beginning with the ink, he still
(The printer) had the presence of mind to change
His operating process when he noticed
That on the wheels the ink had come out strange.

Because the windows of the shack are latticed
The light that falls upon the stationery
Is often interrupted by straight lines
Which shade the etching. Now the words "Dear Mary"
Appear below the engine on one sheet
Followed by a number of other conventional signs,
Among which are "our love," "one kiss," and "sweet."

The clerk then signs his name—his name is Johnson,
But all he signs is Bill, with a large B
Which overflows its boundaries like a Ronson
With too much fluid in it, which you see
Often, and it can burn you, though the *i*
Was very small and had a tiny dot.
The *l*'s were different—the first was high,
The second fairly low. And there was a spot
Of ink at the end of the signature which served
To emphasize that the letter was complete.
On the whole, one could say his writing swerved
More than the average, although it was neat.
He'd used a blue-black ink, a standing pen,
Which now he stuck back in its stand again.

Smiling and sighing, he opened up a drawer
And took an envelope out, which then he sealed
After he'd read the letter three times more
And folded it and put it in. A field
Covered with snow, untouched by man, is what
The envelope resembled, till he placed
A square with perforated edges that
Pictured a white-haired President, who faced
The viewer, in its corner, where it stuck
After he'd kissed its back and held it hard
Against the envelope. Now came the truck
Of the postman "Hello, Jim." "Hello there, Bill."
"I've got this—can you take it?" "Sure, I will!"

Now the snow fell down gently from the sky.
Strange wonder—snow in spring! Bill walked into
The shack again and wrote the letter *I*
Idly upon a sheet of paper. New
Ideas for writing Mary filled his mind,
But he resisted—there was work to do.
For in the distance he could hear the grind
Of the Seventy-Eight, whose engine was half blue;
So, putting on a cap, he went outside
On the tracks side, to wait for it to come.
It was the Seventy-Eight which now supplied
The city with most of its produce, although some
Came in by truck and some was grown in town.
Now it screams closer, and he flags it down.

THE ISLANDS

Triplets
Do you ever think of
   the good times
When my sleeves
You see, the pilot said,
The king offered me the Admiralty
Islands as a reward for the sludge but the
Motors were filled with steamy juice and
Wouldn't start. My friend Harry
Tried to dry them out by opening
The motor cover and letting the hot wind blow
In, all to no avail—so you see
We just sat there, the way
You and your girlfriends did in the
What you say and
                         A child, weak
With fatigue, wandered up to the
Airplane and there was a smell of joss.
We couldn't let that go on on
Flower Island, so Andy hauled this
Kid up to Pilot Lodge where he
Confessed that he had
Other jealous men
Glanced into the air
You have no right
Thing like that—old
Ways forbid but meanwhile
What sunlight and motor not still
Then that smell again—
With just a tiny piece of her we got up
The child smiled
"I wish you steamy joys"
Then I knew
We wouldn't make the islands
I was shivering
Harry's arm was just a stump
The joss had eaten it
As hot nails   opened into blue
The earth had melted away.

84

Inside you I feel a revision
Of all my ideals
Day open like a tin-can—We
Smelled, suddenly,
Some joss   its
Smell was mingled with that
Of wet mud—Harry
Stood up and tried to
Guide the airplane
Closer to the ship—He had
A long pole   looked funny   The captain
Bearded man of fifty-six who
Five days afterwards   ,   we already
Accustomed to
Told Harry   he a "blockbuster" or
"Bookworm"   Then onto
Deck stepped
A Chinese miss
Named "Jolie."

"Sylvia was just a child when I began my career on the
But such a dreamer! she would lean back against her—"
The charms being five
I am happiest
When I am with you
Some say she dropped a baby on the island
What has it all to do
You hurt my prunes again
Let me have a look at it
For five cents a trip you can get the
Whole skedaddle triremed
Stick
You're so sweaty
Because I have no arms
Everything is twice as difficult for me
                for you
Harry put rice all over his face
Picked up the scissors
And acted crazy
But the consul wanted the girl

And said he would have to go back to Zululand
On the next ship.
She was tan and brown and slippery
He had a baby by her anyway.
The baby was named Voss
And fought for the U. S. Navy
At Sarapatee— "I tried to get
It   into the clear."

We moved up
A little closer
    still couldn't make out what
They were saying.   Ed smelled joss
"Is that all they DO out here?"
"Ho, no, Eddie, not at all—
These people are . . ."
Her smell sweet
The sea   lilac of angry fudge

Couldn't keep bringing those
Carpenter tools
                every day
Back to the plane   without
At some time   attracting
The attention of the
Major, who, naturally, would have
Like to know what was
Going on   ·
              found her attractive
Wanting her in his cabin at night
He would find all kinds of ways
Attract her attention   for example
Sending up flags   green
Or red   dark harbor
                        lilypads   ·
Over her door
And along path to her
                    The father
An old man with rice in his ear
Never taken sedative

In eighty-nine years on the island,   once
Made all the cadets wear golden hats
And take them off to her
As she passed . . . And thus he accomplished
He so ardently
Desired? Bee stings
She scratched him
He found her "cute" but
The sergeant, Leonard,
Would often find him
"Not really a disgrace
To the service, but
My God a comment on
Something how true!" lying stretched out
In the purple tide flaked
With dawn spots
Covered with bruises and
Slashed—   "As if she
Were trying
Make a woman out of me, Sergeant.
God!" Innuendoes
He thought of but never said,   as
"You should raise welts on her, Sir"—
A good idea he hadn't
The boycott
Famous old word misused again
And the local nut
Who had gasped with pleasure on half the island

"Promiscuity
Is not attractive—Go home from the dance—"
Not from the native dance!
She was a silver
Blade   and he was like a hammer
Roses   cannon   dawn
Night flushed syringe
"What did you say
We don't have any of those
On this island . . ."

Then
The Colonel took her
Over again
Find his silver eagle attractive
Better than a bug
                    dawn
                        the shore
I wish you hadn't reduced
What? did the milk—
A dog lay   breathing
But half dead
We can't do anything
Invitations   already out

Are you descended from those
People, Voss?
Half

Half a sunset   "fire-tossed horse"
Cannonade   the smell of farts-
Disintegrated by breeze
Come—   Nineteen years I'll be an old woman
Can't abide you
The business parlors
Appealed to him much more
                            that
Green cloth on the tables
"Better than native girls"
More minimal
The sea's light blue wash
"They scratched him up, it was weird
As if they had never seen a man before
On the island . . ."
Said he had a good time
Home sitting on the swing   worst
Old time no plenty come back
   the
Horse farting
Why I could hardly stare a white girl in the face
Shit on calf

Sorry,   I—
                    then realized ridiculous
Talk
Perhaps won't mind doesn't know
                                   I am
Roses, bridge, her forehead
Even a great one
The cow drops
Memory of her name no I white rose I
Send me back you see
Never, Dad
Soldered up
  for repeal
Meanwhile she was running
Wonder how those
Tout-blankety   native girls—
Voss!
Your own mother
No, boy, I'm not going
To sit around while that   !
Am Lieutenant Governor
Greaseball!
Kill him!
Dropped into the sea
When they unwrapped it
Found her earrings
                    and his cloth
"Maple leafs" as well as
The naked body of a sixteen-year-old boy
Completely defaced with scratches
Like a "torpedo"
"When I think that that might
Have happened to me"—
Sunlight
Crutches
Someone named "Lillian Liberty"

Vile old iron ways

THE DEPARTURE FROM HYDRA

As I was walking home just now, from seeing
Margaret and Norris off (though Peter,
An Englishman whom Norris had met yesterday,
Went back to change his clothes, and missed the boat)
As I came home along the little street
Without a name on which the only theatre,
The movie theatre, on Hydra is,
Called "The Gardenia" or just plain "Gardenia,"
The street which they today are tearing up
And carrying new stones in to replace
The ones they're tearing up, though it may be
They are the same stones, put in different order
Or in a different way, as I was walking,
With the heat of the day just over, at five-thirty,
I felt quite good, but then felt an awareness
Of something in my legs that might be painful
And then of some slight tension in my jaws
And slight pains in my head; instead of despairing
And giving all thought of pleasure up, I felt
That if I could write down all that I felt
As I came walking there, that that would be
A pleasure also, and with solidity.
I passed a mule—some men were loading up
His fellow-mule with packets—and I stared
At his wide eyes and his long hard flat nose
Or face, at which he turned away his eyes
And stamped his right hoof nervously. I felt
Guilty, a member of a higher species
Deliberately using my power against
A natural inferior because
Really I was afraid that he might kick
When I came past; but when he seemed upset
Then I felt guilty. Then I looked ahead
And saw a view of houses on the hill,
Particularly noticing one red one
And thinking, Yes, that is a part of what
I feel, of the variety of this walk;
Then my mind blurred somewhat, I turned and came

Down this small narrow alley to my home.
As I came in, reviewing the ideas
Which had occured to me throughout my walk,
It suddenly came to me that maybe Peter
Had missed the Athens boat deliberately;
After all, Margaret was not sure that she
Wanted to accompany him and Norris
On a walking trip on Poros, and Norris had said
He wanted to stay with Margaret, so that Peter
Was disappointed, since he and Norris had planned
That very morning to take such a walking trip,
And he, Peter, had been the most excited
Of all, about it. But now since Margaret and Norris
Were going into Athens, what was there for Peter
To do, why should he take the boat at all,
Even though he'd planned to, to stop at Poros?
Except, of course, to act on some marginal chance
That Norris might get off with him and walk,
Or on the strength of previous expectations,
Emotional impetus lingering. If not,
Perhaps his going to change was just an excuse
To avoid an actual confrontation with Norris
In which he would have to say, "No, I'm not going
Unless you'll come on the walking trip!" but he knew,
Peter, that Norris wanted to stay with Margaret
And that therefore speaking to him would only result
In a little pain and confusion, since both were quite drunk,
Having planned their trip to Poros over beer all morning;
And also, of course, it might result in his getting,
In spite of himself, on the boat, by the talk confused
And not thinking clearly (whereas if he walked away
He had only, really, to wait till the boat had left—
Then he could come back down and think it over,
Surely to find he didn't regret too much
Not getting the boat, because after all the reason
He'd wanted to take the boat had long been gone).
For a human situation often leads
People to do things that they don't desire
At all, but they find that what they did desire
Has somehow led them to this situation

In which not to do that which is proposed
Seems inconsistent, hostile, or insane,
Though much more often very unfriendly; then too
Sometimes it chiefly is a lack of time
To explain how things have changed that leads one, waving
One's hands, aboard a ship that bodes one ill.
To walk away as Peter did is one way
Of avoiding such situations—another way
Is never to deceive or have high hopes
For foolish things; to be straight with oneself,
With one's own body, nature, and society,
To cast off everything that is not clear
And definite, and move toward one desire
After another, with no afterthoughts.
Living in this way one avoids the sudden
Transports of excitement Peter felt
When Norris mentioned a Poros walking tour.
For surely if Peter's natural desires
Had all been satisfied, if his life were running
Smoothly sexually, and if his health
Were excellent and his work going well,
He scarcely would have gotten so excited
At the mere thought of walking around Poros;
This sort of thing, however, often happens
To people from Northern countries, not just Peter,
And perhaps if one is English, Norse, or Swedish,
Danish, Finnish, Swiss, or North American,
One cannot avoid a certain amount of tension,
A certain quavering in the hand which reaches
For a ripe peach or the shoulder of a girl,
One whom, as one walks back from going swimming,
One thinks that one could eat, she's so delicious,
But only thinks it for a little while
(This thought itself is such a Northern one!
A Southerner would think about a place
Where he could go and jump on top of her)—
In any case, then, Northerners find it hard
To avoid such sudden excitements, but the English,
And especially the upper class, are worst of all,
Because besides their climate that's oppressed them

There's also been a restrictive upbringing,
Manners around the house perhaps too severe
For children—I am speaking of those English
Who escape from "class" and become bright or artistic,
The ones one sees on places like this island.
(These sudden outbursts of enthusiasm, of course,
Are often much admired by other people,
Particularly some not very smart ones,
Who think however they're very sensitive
And what they most admire is "vitality"
Which they think things like outbursts are a sign of,
And they can bore you far into the night
With telling you how wonderful some Dane
Or Norsky is, when you could be asleep
Dreaming of satisfying your desires
With persons who are always very warm,
Tender, and exciting—but, awake!
They're talking still, and though your sickly smile
Gets sicklier every moment, they go on:
"Hans suddenly got the idea to
Inundate Denmark. He is wonderful!"
"Oh, marvelous! Where does one go to meet him?"
"I'll give you his address. He has a farm
Where he stays in the summer; he loves animals,
But sometimes when he drinks a lot he beats them
And says that he can understand their language."
"How marvelous!" "And here's his city address:
Beschtungen aber Bass Gehundenweiss
996." "Goodnight." But Peter is
Not an exaggerated case like that,
And not a nagging bore who talks of such
People, but he has "outbursts" all the same.
It is true, in a sense these outbursts are
Difficult to discriminate from real
Vitality, which everyone esteems
These days because of man's oppressed position
In modern society, which saps his strength
And makes him want to do what everyone else does,
Whereas some man who says, "Let's pitch the glasses
Against the lamppost" is likely to be praised

By some low-IQ person who is there
As being really vital, ah he's wonderful.
Vitality, however, usually
Appeals to an answering vital force in others
And brings about making love or great events,
Or it at least gives pleasure—I can't judge
Vitality in any way but the way
It gives me pleasure, for if I do not get
Pleasure from life, of which vitality
Is just the liquid form, then what am I
And who cares what I say? I for one don't.
Therefore I judge vitality that way.)
But Peter, after having this idea
Of a walking trip on Poros, must have felt
That in walking around in the sun all day on an island
About which he knew nothing, there might come
Some insight to him or some relaxation,
Some feeling the way an Italian feels all the time,
Or perhaps not, perhaps he never does;
Peter at any rate was probably not
Conscious of an Italian at the time
He thought with pleasure about the walk on Poros,
But there he was, faced with Norris and Margaret
An hour before the boat came in, and Norris
Was saying "Maybe not." One mistake of Peter,
Or, rather, difficulty, a common one
In such enthusiasms, is that since
One's enthusiasm is motivated by submerged
Feelings and so its object isn't clear
To anyone, it is most likely that
Though they respond excitedly at first,
Partly because excitement is so communicable,
Others, when they think over what you've planned,
Will see it in a greyer light, unless of course
They have the same neuroses that you have,
In which case a whole lifetime might be built
Upon one of these outbursts. Norris, probably,
In drinking with Peter, wanted more than anything
To be agreeable, whereas Peter wanted
To "do" something unusual, not necessarily

94

Pleasing to Norris, not necessarily displeasing;
Norris, I should imagine, then, once he
Was out of Peter's company, since he'd known him
A very short time, was lacking the chief impulse
That motivated him when he agreed
To take a tour with Peter; therefore Margaret,
Speaking to Norris when he was alone
And saying she did not want to take the trip,
Found he immediately agreed with her,
Expressed some doubts at least, and said all right,
The trip was off then, he'd explain to Peter;
Peter, of course, was very surprised by this,
But still he must have been used to it because
The way that Norris and Margaret acted was based
On laws of human conduct which endure;
And since that outburst surely was not his first,
Peter was probably accustomed to
That sort of outcome of his impulses
And said to himself, "Ah, they don't understand,"
But probably knew inside that there was something
Seriously the matter with him. So when he left
The table and said, "I'm going to get my things,"
It was with a certain tension that he left,
Indicative of the fact he'd not come back,
And of the fact that he knew he would not avoid
Self-doubts because he avoided the useless boat trip;
Of course he wouldn't think he should have gone
But wonder why things had been the way they were.
It was these deeper worries in his mind,
I think, that kept him from leaving even sooner
With the same excuse, rather than a hope that Norris
Would change his mind again. Deep thoughts make helpless
Men for small undertakings. Well, perhaps
The last is speculation, but the rest
Seems surely true. I smiled, and closed the door.

A Selected List of Evergreen Books

If your bookseller doesn't have these books, you may order them by writing to Order Dept., Grove Press, Inc., 80 University Place, New York, New York 10003. Please enclose cash and add 25¢ for postage and handling.